EXCELSIOR

the Lost Pioneer

EXCELSIOR
the Lost Pioneer

SECOND EDITION

T.J. Liversidge

authorHOUSE®

AuthorHouse™ UK
1663 Liberty Drive
Bloomington, IN 47403 USA
www.authorhouse.co.uk
Phone: 0800.197.4150

Published by AuthorHouse 04/14/2015

ISBN: 978-1-5049-4101-3 (sc)
ISBN: 978-1-5049-4102-0 (e)

Print information available on the last page.

Excelsior motorcycles the story of a true pioneer in British motorcycle production.

Many people if asked will know of the great pioneers of the motorcycle industry here in the UK. The likes of Norton, Triumph and BSA have all had their stories document many times. Unfortunately if asked about the part that Excelsior motorcycles had played in this illustrious history you would probably be met with a blank expression. As the majority of people these days have never heard of the Excelsior motorcycle. Let alone know of the companies link to the motorcycling history of Britain. So I decided to write this book to help put the Excelsior motorcycle back in the public's conciseness. Even if its only the motorcycle fraternity. This rewrite of my earlier book has taken some time to comply I hope that book will be well received by all who read it. So here is the story of excelsior motorcycles of Tysely Birmingham UK.

We open the pages of Excelsiors history in middle of queen Victoria's reign the British Isles were in the grips of one of the fastest expansions of industrial technology in its history. The old Britain based on agriculture was being swept away, as coal and iron were harnessed in vast quantities to fuel this growth. From these material assets British industry would grow at ever increasing circles.

Meanwhile at the same time as this momentous growth in industry many of our cities would also start to grow at an alarming rate as more and more people made their way to them in search of employment. Hopefully in one of the numerous new factories or workshops springing up within them. Among the new factories found in the city of Coventry, they would have found a small factory that was involved with the manufacturing of parts for the new bicycle industry. Here excelsior would take its first tentative steps toward greater things. This new factory at 78 Much park street in Coventry was the joint conception of three former employees of Britain's first bicycle manufacturer James Starley of Coventry. They were Messrs Bayliss, Thomas and Slaughter. Together they would set up the new business initially for the supply of spares for bicycles, as well as carry out subcontract work for James Starley among others.

The year the company was formed was 1874. This year would see the birth of the company that would expand at an amazing rate over the next ten years. This small initial factory that comprised of 3 former cottages knocked into a single unit for the purpose of manufacturing. This practice was not to uncommon a practice in those days. As what seemed to be the norm at this time no one stood still for long and within a couple of years Bayliss and Thomas would find themselves on their own and producing bicycles of their own design. Quite why Slaughter had left the company I don't know but it was to have very little impact on the newly named company of Bayliss and Thomas. In fact before long the range of products leaving much park street would grow to include perambulators and penny farthings or Ordinaries to give them their proper name.

ESTABLISHED 1874. THE OLDEST FIRM IN COVENTRY WITH ONE EXCEPTION.

SEASON, 1881.

Bayliss, Thomas & Co.,

PATENTEES & MANUFACTURERS OF

The World~Renowned

EXCELSIOR

Bicycles & Tricycles

CARRIAGE AND PERAMBULATOR

India~Rubber Tyred Wheels.

EXCELSIOR WORKS,

LOWER FORD ST., COVENTRY.

PRINTED BY ILIFFE & SON, SMITHFORD STREET, COVENTRY.

As can be seen on this early advertisement from Bayliss and Thomas. They wasted no time increasing the range of products.

As the orders grew so did the new company as it found its self squeezed into the cramped conditions of much park street. So it was in 1880 the company would move to a new purpose built factory at 80 Lower ford street Coventry. Now the company was able to expand the business even greater. By now Bayliss and Thomas were looking for a new brand name for the new business. They were to finally decide on Excelsior. This name was derived from a poem by Henry Longfellow about an mountaineer. The company badge depicted a young man waving a flag on top of a mountain. This badge would be kept as the company icon, and was to be found on machines they produced right up until the companies demise.

The new works as well as the company would carry this new name. known as the Excelsior works. This would lead on inevitably to more rapid growth. Before very long the scope and range of products leaving the lower ford street works had tripled. As the factory grew so did its work force. Giving greater employment to the surrounding area.

This in turn would lead to more businesses benefiting from excelsiors good fortune. Generating more wealth for Coventry. Even with this new much larger factory excelsior still would have to sub contract a lot of work out to other companies in Coventry. Including suppliers for all the raw materials that the company now needed. Along with specialists such as rust proofing steel parts, manufactured ball bearings, steel tubing and rubber for the tyres to name but a few. I have managed to get hold of a copy of a very early of a drawing print of the new lower ford street sight. This you will find on the next page. Do take into account the age of this picture when viewing it. As the quality isn't at its best. I decided to included this picture as it does give a very good idea of the size of the lower ford street works. This in turn lets you realise how big the company had grown by this time.

As you can see from this early print the new factory was very impressive. An amazing achievement to transform the company in such a short period of time. Obviously the production at these new works would match the size of the premises.

Innovation was the key to the companies rapid expansion one of the most important for bicycle manufacture was the DEHF or duplex Excelsior hollow forks. This would greatly reduce the over all weight of the new bicycles leaving the Excelsior works. In previous models the forks had been constructed from solid steel so by simply changing to steel tubing the machine constructed would have its weight greatly reduced. Which of course made the life of the cyclist a lot easier.

From the onset of the first frames constructed by Excelsior would use the braised lug type of construction This technique would stay in continued use through out the entire life of the company.

All the bicycles leaving lower ford street would be built to include the same long levity components in them. These included double races of ball bearings on all the spindles that were set into drilled perforated steel bands. As well as hardened recesses cut into the frame its self. Each wheel crank would be fitted with adjustable bearings to insure longevity of life for these components too. All bearings would be sealed with dust caps as well to prevent the ingress of dust and dirt and to act as a grease seal too. Cranks would be locked in place with D shaped wedges. Main backbones of the bicycles were constructed of 13/8 diameter steel tubing with a perfect taper to the rear. Always striving to offer the best quality that they could excelsior cycles were considered among the top quality available at this time. With an attention to details such as I have just mentioned you can see why.

The number one ordinary was undoubtedly the main back bone of production in the early years. There would follow many variants including tricycles among them the number one tricycle this would provide the most versatile design. Used by the British postal service among others because of its ability to fit through narrow passages. As well as bicycles and tricycles production included many smaller items that the owners would find useful. Bicycle alarms, bells, shoes and speedometer to name a few. The bicycles would be joined by other products such as perambulators and invalid carriages would also be available.

OUR BOYS' EXCELSIOR.

The demand for a machine, as above, having greatly increased, we have given the same our special attention, and are enabled to supply a light, strong, and serviceable Bicycle, at the following low

PRICES.

Inside Measurement of Leg.	Front Wheel Diameter.	£ s. d.
22-in., 23-in., 24-in. ..	30-in., 32-in., 34-in. ..	6 10 0
25-in. 26-in., 27-in. ..	36-in., 38-in., 40-in. ..	7 0 0

The pattern is the same as our " Excelsior," complete with Saddle, Pedals, Spanner, and Oil Can. Fitted with front wheel Brake.

THE CHILD'S TRICYCLE.

	SIZE.		£ s. d.
For Children, age 4 to 7 years,	22in. back wheel, 12in. front whee		3 3 0
	24in. ,,	12in. ,,	3 13 6
7 to 10 ,,	25in. ,,	14in. ,,	4 4 0
,, 10 and upwards,	30in. ,,	14in. ,,	In proportion

With in the space of one year excelsior would find that the production had out grown even the new works at lower ford street. So in 1881 an extension to the works was added. This would doubled the size of floor space available for production. This intern would enabled the company to almost triple their production by 1882. The company had come a long way in just eight years. Britain was booming and excelsior were helping by lead the way in bicycle manufacturing. In fact later that year the company was acknowledged as among the leading exporters in Coventry. Other features included on the new machines included the rust proofing of all steel parts. This work was to be carried out by another Coventry based company J. Douglas and co of 287-295 Stoney station road Coventry. This company was one of the many companies used by excelsior to provide specialist expertise that excelsior at this time were unable to provide for themselves. With the continuous expansion excelsior would be adding to the range of machines available from lower ford street all the time. One of the new machines was called the Sociable, best described as a cross between a tandem and a cart. Built with comfort in mind for both the rider and passenger. As promenading was very much in fashion by this point. This was the Victorian equivalent of driving your flash sports car along the promenade so as you can show it off. The sociable appeared from the front like two large wheels with a pair of seats set between them. Drive for the machine was taken of the left side wheel, this was by means of a rather clever design that was incorporated into the drive mechanism of this machine. Not a normal linked chain as most other bicycles used or direct wheel drive as found on the ordinaries. No not for the sociable it would have a specially designed system. That Incorporated the pedal gear. Looking not to unlike modern bicycle gearing. This will become apparent on this page. As you can to see from the photo.

As can be seen in the picture above it was a very complicated piece of engineering. More like a series of inter linked cogs rather than the traditional chain drive we know today.

There were many such oddity's available from all manufactures at this time as every one tried to find that perfect bicycle design that in turn would give them the accolade and orders they wanted.

These bicycles were also considered to have the latest technology, prices reflected this at the time for example.

The number 1 tricycle would set you back from £16 16s to £17 6s.

The prices of the bicycles varied Depending on the size of the drive wheel on the machine you purchased. Optional extras included nickel plating to many exposed parts this would add an extra £5 to the cost of the machine. The nickel plating would be carried out in house at the lower ford street works. This plating plant would help to bring in extra revenue as a subcontracting arm of the company. As would the machine shop in providing spares for the excelsior range and offering subcontracting to other manufacturing companies in Coventry and further afield. Even though the Excelsior name had now become well known and linked to the Coventry based company, several other companies around the world also used Excelsior as their trade name at this time. Including an American company that were also producing bicycles. So to allow sales of the Coventry built machines in the USA it was decided the old trade name of Bayliss Thomas and co would be used on machines exported to America. The main importer of Bayliss and Thomas bicycles into the united states was Messrs Cunningham and co. of Boston, under the trade name of Harvard. By now Excelsior were gaining a world wide reputation for excellence. This in turn led to rapid turn over of orders for their machines. By now more modern looking bicycles were being designed.

So by 1885 the standard bicycle lay out that we know today had been developed. Known as the safety bicycle and would be produced by many companies including Excelsior. This standardization of the bicycle would lead to the demise of the old fashioned larger wheeled machines such as the ordinary. The ordinaries were very dangerous to ride compared to the new safety bicycle. After all you were perched up high on a wheel so it would be a long fall down. So I guess they were not missed for to long. On the other hand the tricycles would carry on along side the safety bicycles for some time to come.

From the very earliest days bicycles built by Excelsior would find their way on to the race track. Here are some examples of the early days of bicycle racing involving excelsior.

on the 17th of may 1880 a Mr A.M.Tooney would record a win on an Excelsior D.E.H.F with a 56 inch wheel. At the all Irish championships.

The same model was reported to be the favourite machine of the American bicycle team touring the UK in that same year. Again in 1881 this time on a tricycle Excelsior would gain the honours in the 10 mile tricycle championship. Held at the Belgrave grounds at Liecester on the 19th of April. The Winning rider this time was a Mr S. Corbet completing the course in 42 minutes and 54 seconds. Not at all bad going on a tricycle.

At first most products available from the new lower ford street factory would be aimed at the well off upper classes As is evident by the prices list on the next page. As the prices are with out a doubt way above the yearly wage earned by many British workers at this time. Soon this early customer base would expand as new customers such as the postal office would show interest in the Excelsior machines. Of course with mass production would come lower priced machines bring them with in reach of more people.

Mean while this is a picture of a sociable one of the many tricycles produced at lower ford street, by Bayliss and Thomas.

I have seen this particular example many times. It is a very fine example of a Victorian tricycle.

This machine has been renovated to a very high standard. It is most agile and surprisingly fast when in use.

A novel way to ride a bicycle made for two. Certainly more comfortable than the traditional tandem's. Which Excelsior also produced in great quantities.

I would say these new supper tricycles were extremely expensive in there day. Even more so today as they are now very rare beasts indeed.

It is evident that the Excelsior company had by now become masters in engineering to the highest standards of the day. With their ever increasing portfolio of products coming out of lower ford street.

List of Prices of the "Excelsior" Bicycles.

Length of Leg Inside Measurement to sole of foot.	Diameter of Front Wheel.	Diameter of Back Wheel	Duplex and Stanley "Excelsior" Hollow Fk. with Ball Bearings, Roadster, Semi Racer and Racer.	Duplex "Excelsior," No. 1. Duplex Semi Racer. Duplex Racer.	The Duplex "Excelsior" No. 2.	The "Excelsior" No. 1.	The "Excelsior" No. 2.
Inches	Inches.	Inches.	£ s. d.	£ s. d.	£ s. d.	£ s. d.	£ s. d.
28	42	16	13 10 0	12 10 0	11 10 0	10 10 0	8 10 0
29	44	16	14 0 0	13 0 0	12 0 0	11 0 0	9 0 0
30	46	16	14 10 0	13 10 0	12 10 0	11 10 0	9 10 0
31	48	16	15 0 0	14 0 0	13 0 0	12 0 0	10 0 0
32	50	18	15 10 0	14 10 0	13 10 0	12 10 0	10 10 0
33	52	18	16 0 0	15 0 0	14 0 0	13 0 0	11 0 0
34	54	18	16 10 0	15 10 0	14 10 0	13 10 0	11 10 0
35	56	18	17 0 0	16 0 0	15 0 0	14 0 0	12 0 0
36	58	18	17 10 0	16 10 0	15 10 0	14 10 0	12 10 0
37	60	18	18 0 0	17 0 0	16 0 0	15 0 0	13 0 0

Ball Bearings to Back Wheel, 10s. extra.

Half Bright, Bright Head, front and back Fork Ends, Step and part of back bone for dismounting, 15s. extra. All Bright, less Felloes, 30/-. Felloes, 10/- extra

Bright Parts Plated, viz.—Hubbs, Nipples, Spokes, Cranks, Head, Handle-bar, Spring, Slide, and part of backbone, 40/- extra.

All Plated Except Rims, £4 10s. extra. Rims, 10/- extra.

prices for Excelsior bicycles

NICKEL PLATING.

Nickel-plated machines having found great favour amongst our numerous customers, we have added to our Plant one of Weston's Patent Dynamo Electric Machines with all appliances, whereby we are enabled to guarantee the quality and durability of the Nickel-plating as applied to our Machines. Nickel-plating of every description. Estimates given.

Route to Messrs. Bayliss, Thomas & Co.'s Works.

BAYLISS, THOMAS & C⁰ BICYCLE MANUFACTURERS **COVENTRY**

Messrs. B. T. & Co. will be pleased to take charge of Bicycles, render any aid, or give any information to Bicyclists passing through the City, free of charge.

Each Machine is etched on the Spring, thus

Terms—*Nett Cash. Post Office Orders or Cheques to accompany Order or on Receipt of Invoice.*
Photos. of any of our Machines, 3 stamps each.   Lists, 1 stamp.

CARRIAGE.—Each Machine is packed in crate, and sent per goods train; or, per passenger train, if desired.
CRATES being charged under cost price, viz.: Bicycle, 3/-; Tricycle, 4/-; are not returnable.

The new world concept

As the end of the 19th century was drawing to a close in 1896 Excelsior would produce possibly the last great break through in two wheeled transport. That year at the Crystal palace show venue the trade fair would see Excelsior offer the first British built motorcycle for sale to the general public. There had been a few prototypes built previously but this was the first mass produced machine to come on the market.

It was reported at the time that next to the motorized machine the Excelsior sales team had placed a notice that read. Take me for a ride if you dare! One can only surmise the offer was taken up by a good many people. As the out come is plain to see today as they say it was a great page in the book of history. Among the earlier machines in Excelsiors motorcycle range were machines fitted with a 996 cc Minerva engine. Other machines with engines built by other manufacturers to choose from would shortly follow. These would include DE Dion, MMC and possibly the largest single cylinder machines ever built in the UK. Fitted with a 850 cc Condor engine. These were also built in Coventry.

With the new emphasis on building motorized machines in 1910 the company decided to change its name to the Excelsior motor company limited. For the time being production would continue at the lower ford street works.

Unfortunately the first world war would soon be raging across Europe and along with every one else Excelsior would be expected to do its bit. Among the war orders would be one from the old imperial Russian army for a number of machines with large engines fitted with side car outfits. Powered by Jap v twin engines built by

John Alfred Prestwich of Tottenham north London. These were the largest engines available to Excelsior at the time. In fact the Jap company had already gained a good reputation for reliability and sound engineering.

So most British manufactures during this period of time built machines with Jap engines fitted. The JAP company was originally set up in 1895 as a cinematographic equipment manufacturer. Before long the company had built its first motorcycle engine. Which was put into production by1903. This first engine was a 293 cc engine. Between 1904 and 1909 the Jap factory also built its own line of motorcycles. Though John Prestwich soon realized his companies future lay with engine manufacture. So the motorcycle line was dropped from production.

Within a very short time Excelsior would be joined by a periphery of other motorcycle manufactures in motorcycle production. Among them some of the most well recognized manufactures from our motorcycling history. Including Coventry eagle, Calphorp, Majestic, Matchless, Brough superior, Rex-acme, Wolf and Zenith. With the introduction of these and other motorcycle producers the British motorcycle industry had come of age. The company would continue with the manufacture of excelsior motorcycles up to and including the first world war. With the end of the first world war would also come the end of motorcycle manufacture by Excelsior in Coventry.

During the first world war excelsior had under gone tremendous changes. As well as a series of losses including the loss of a large Russian imperial army order. Brought about because of the revolution. This would give the company financial problems, as a large number of the motorcycles in the order had already been completed and shipped over to Russia.. Faced with the prospect of financial ruin the board reluctantly decided it was time to sell the company. So it was that in 1921 the company was sold to R. Walker and son of Birmingham. Formerly one of Excelsiors sub contractors. So now the company would move to Kings Street Tysely Birmingham.

Francis Barnett would take over the old Excelsior works at lower ford street Coventry producing their own motorcycles.

The walkers Reginald and son Eric would register the new company as the Excelsior motor co Ltd. During their time in charge they will over see the introduction of some of the more well known models to be produced under the British Excelsior name.

Even though the new kings road factory would be a lot smaller than the one occupied in Lower ford street production would concentrate on quality light weight machines. While incorporating the production of some early auto mobiles.

During the early days at Kings road engines would still be sourced externally as the Walkers had no machine tooling for engine production at kings road. Among the engine builders used in the new factory were Villiers, Blackburn and JAP.

Here is a prime example of a 1920s excelsior with JAP engine.

These new engines would enable the new company the chance to be offered a wide range of machines to build. As the list that follows will demonstrate.

Listed at the time as Excelsiors most popular models in production were.

Model number 1. This machine had a 147 cc two stroke Villiers engine with a bore of 55 mm and a stroke of 62 mm. Capable of developing just one and three quarters horse power.

Model number 2. Was also built by Villiers and had 247 cc with a stoke of 70 mm and bore of 67 mm.

Once again a single cylinder two stroke engine that actually was less powerful in developing only one and a half horse power.

Model number 3. A single cylinder four stroke engine of 348cc. With a bore of 71 mm and stroke of 88mm.developing up to two and three quarters horse power. This was a Blackburn side valve engine.

Model number4. A thumping 770cc v twin built by JAP with bores of 76mm and strokes of 85mm. Developing six horse power.

Model number 5. this was the largest engine used in an Excelsior at this time a whopping 976cc v twin built once again by JAP. With bores and strokes of 85mm. Capable of developing 8 horse power.

As well as these a fore mentioned machines each year new models would join the production at Excelsior. These included in 1924 a 600cc side valve and 2 new 545 cc models one for racing and one with a longer stroke for side car use.

By 1925 a 173cc model with a Blackburn engine and a 349cc fitted with a Bradshaw engine model were added to the production line. By 1925 excelsior had taken their first TT trophy on a B14 model. This machine went on to be the most popular sales model that year. This machine would herald the beginnings of a close association with the race track.

Then as the company entered 1926 they would see the introduction of a smaller general range of machines due to the great depression and a sales slump.

Fortunately by 1927 the company seemed to be edging forward again. Two new models would join the range during this year a new JAP engine of 347cc and a 490cc Villiers engine were to be found in use.

1928 gave a new two stroke machine with a 247cc engine. Two stroke engines were proving ever more popular by this time.

In 1931 the famous Universal model was launched with a 98cc Villiers engine and cost just 14 guineas easily the cheapest bike of its type available. According to advertisements of the day.

There would also be a special much cheaper machine built during the 1920s as at this time the great depression was eating into all aspects of industry not just in the UK but all over the world. With this in mind the model O or minor was born. A simple single loop frame held a small Villiers 98cc midget engine. The petrol tank was a simple pressed steel triangle type of construction. Many companies at this time were producing these so called poverty models as a means to keep their companies going through the lean times. These simple machines would act as a means of keeping the work force busy, even if orders were lean for the other machines in the range.

Amazingly hand in hand with these simple machines Excelsior would still work on new projects for future production. One such research and development project was the Viking. This fully enclosed machine with stream lined tin wear was really quite advanced for its day. The engine was a joint adventure with Villiers. Not only was it a two stroke that was water cooled, the oil was not delivered to the cylinder in the time Honoured way via petrol/oil mixing. No this engine had an oil governance system that relied on engine pressure in the crank to draw the oil into the cylinder and other working parts of the engine. Unfortunately this technique was to prove vulnerable to drops in pressure caused by gasket leaks or seals. So the Viking only had a short production run.

By now along side the standard machines offered by Excelsior they also built a number of Tradesman vehicles. The main two models were the traditional boxed side car arrangement to be fitted to your existing motorcycle. As well as quirky little combination of car and motorcycle. Having two wheels on the front set either side of a large enclosed box for carting goods in. the engine was mounted under the drivers seat just behind the box. This run a chain drive to a single back wheel. And steerage was by means of a steering wheel. Not the usual handle bars associated with motorcycles. How it handled is any bodies guess but speed certainly wasn't an option.

Of course this only gives you a small insight into the range of products that by now were being produced at the kings road Excelsior works.

As well as the motorcycles produced at kings road just prior to the second world war a number of auto mobiles were also built to order under the Bayliss Thomas trade name. This was because there was already a company in Belgium that used the Excelsior name on cars it built. The first experimental vehicle was produced much earlier in 1919 this was an three wheeled auto mobile that never got past the prototype stage. Three years later four wheeled models were released for sale. These four wheeled models were as follows. 10.8 this model was also fitted with a simplex engine and a three speed gear box. Manufactured between 1922 and 1924. described as a sliding door saloon. Available in two and four seated versions.

The 11/22 this was a four seated touring car. That was built by excelsior between 1924 and 1927. fitted with a simplex engine and only available with back brakes until 1927, at which time front brakes were also fitted as standard.

The 12/12 model was fitted with a 1500cc meadows engine. And was available in both four and six seated versions. This car also had to wait until 1927 for its full set of brakes. But it had a three speed gear box from the onset of production. Built between 1925 and 1927.

13/13 a coupé model available with four or six seats. A meadows 1795 cc engine and a four speed gear box was standard on this model.

It is believed that excelsior of Birmingham produced auto mobiles until 1930 the last models being registered in 1931. only around a thousand cars were built during this period of time.

After this last auto mobile had been produced, kings road would concentrated on its production on motorcycles.

Not just auto mobiles were available by now excelsior offered other products. These were also built along side the cars and motorcycles such as outboard engines and generators. Some of these products would carry on in production almost as long as the motorcycles. By now the new company had made a name for its self to rival that of the old Coventry predecessor.

As the 1920s were drawing to a close excelsior found that they and their machines were getting more involved with the competition side of the industry.

From humble beginnings on ultra light weight machines they would go on to produce arguably the finest motorcycle to leave the kings road works. These race inspired machines are still among some of the most sort after machines in the world today.

Here is an advert from 1929 showing the winning machine with its rider Stanley Crabtree. Crabtree was to become one of the centre players in the Excelsior motorcycle race team over the next ten years. As you can see Excelsior were in top form as far as the light weight class race machines were concerned.

The company would soon monopolies on these great track successes. Along side the new racing machine a new line of motorcycles would be developed using the successes gained on the track to guide the design of the new road machines.

In fact By 1931 excelsiors competition team had managed to take the 100 mile endurance speed trophy. This would continue be held by excelsior until 1933. Among other early racing machines built by excelsior was a 173 cc machine fitted with Blackburne engine. Further wins on this ultra light weight machine would inspire excelsior to create a mechanical marvel. In fact that would be exactly the name used by excelsior for the new machine.

The mechanical marvel would be a joint design venture between Eric walker of excelsior and Ike hatch of the engine manufacturers Blackburn's of Great Brook ham in Surrey.

This entirely new machine would be built around a completely new type of engine. Every thing about the mechanical marvel was state of the art for the 1930s. The heart of the new machine would be the Incredibly complicated 250 cc single cylinder engine. This engine would have valves operated by a complicated twin cam set up. Using sliding dog gears off of the rocker arms, these were in turn operated by forged connection rods that ran up the outside of the engine. The pistons were made from hiduminium light alloy and incorporated needle bearings. The engine would have twin inlet ports and carburettors arranged across the rear of the engine. All of the engines for these machines were to be built by Blackburn's at there brook ham factory, as Excelsior had no in house facilities for engine building at this time. Early indications were very favourable as the first machines would be factory racers.

Picked to ride the marvel the first time would be Syd Gleave and Wall Hadley. The venue the 1933 TT light weight class. By the end of the first lap Hadley had taken first place position team mate Syd Gleave was found in second place. Unfortunately Hadley's machine with 20 miles still to go on the final lap broke down. This left the way open for his team mate Syd Gleave. He still managed a very good time Gleave even achieved a first positioning. This for a small company such as Excelsior was an amazing achievement for their new machine on its first outing. Bolstered up by their win on the marvel Excelsior eagerly awaited the next season.

Unfortunately fate would be against Excelsiors new prodigy this would prove to be the mechanical marvels only win, as a series of misfortunes were about to befall the machine. This would start with

Blackburn's unavailability to service the new engines at the end of the 1933 season.

The Blackburn works were in trouble leading to their closure by 1935. With the new race season drawing ever nearer Excelsior decided to offer the work of servicing the engines to one of their riders Eric Feinhough. Unfortunately he had limited experience at this type of work. So together with his assistant Francis Beart they tried their best to work on the engines. Unfortunately they would make a number of very serious mistakes the greatest being drilling out the plug holes on all 6 of the marvel engines that Excelsior had in stock. In fact they were the only engines of this type in the world at this time. This one mistake left the exhaust guides vulnerable, as they were supplied with their own separate supply of oil this meant the plugs had to be shielded to prevent them from oiling up. Drilling out the plug holes they effectively removed these shields. At this point Excelsior had some really good luck that happened to come their way. In the form of an exceptional Australian engineer called Alan Bruce. Bruce was much more than an engineer he had also built and raced a number of motorcycles to his own design. His most note worthy success being the gaining of the land speed record on a Rudge machine he helped to design. Initially Bruce had entered the Excelsior works as a guest engineer for shell oils. Eric Walker soon approached him with an offer to help rebuild the marvel engines. After taking up the offer Bruce soon had the engines in working order, no mean feat has the excelsior factory's machine tooling was very limited. Even with Bruce breathing new life into the engines they never were 100% after the Feinhough fiasco. So in 1934 the team would only managed a sixth placement at the TT. Still very impressed with Bruce's obvious abilities Eric Walker offered him the position of technical director in charge of the race department a position he would prove to excel at.

Leaving the marvel behind them the company under the steward ship of Eric Walker and Alan Bruce would now develop an entirely new range of middle and light weight machines.

So would begin a new chapter in excelsiors history one in which they would climb to the top pinnacle of their production, with in house designs wining out like never before.

Based around the single cylinder engine developed by Ike hatch and Eric walker. The range of machines available would be from 250cc to 500cc.

The most exceptional machine that was distend to stand out as excelsiors number one achievement would undoubtedly be the 250cc Manxman. This machine would have many of the attributes developed with the marvel. The most noticeable exception being the change in the cam operating system found in the new Manxman engine.

The new engine had a bevel driven single over head cam with 2 valves in the first models to be released in1935. This model would soon be super seeded in 1936 by a twin cam 4 valve model. So complication was begging to be excelsiors hallmark. This new 4 valve model was entered for that years TT races and managed to gain a second place in the light weight race. This would be An achievement repeated the following year in 1937. Development of the Manxman engine would continue under Alan Bruce with the assistance of Tyrell smith and S.woods. Now we find a very special machine was being developed for the senior TT. This would be a 500cc version of the Manxman. Development on this machine would start in 1938. it is believed that only 10 or even less of these specials were ever built. Engine numbers had the prefix GJD and would be offered to a select few customers. The first prototype was shown to these selected customers at the earls court show in 1938. This machine was the JR15 fitted with engine number GJD99. This engine had been built by Tyrell smith while Alan Bruce had worked on improvements to the 4 valve head. This work on the head was to alleviate a problem the bike had with spark plugs. As the exhaust port was situated next to the plug on the left hand side of the head it gave a short life for the spark plug.

So Bruce would redesigned the head with a right hand port, cast in bronze this cured the spark plug problem. The new engine with its right hand port was numbered GJA100. This engine was put into a frame and thrashed around Donnington park circuit. As well as under going lengthy road testing. In fact Tyrell-smith road the bike the 19 miles home to Coventry from the excelsior works one night in just 14 minutes. When Eric walker learned of this he ordered that all new Manxman machines should be fitted with the new bronze right ported head. These new bronze heads were cast for excelsior by Harry Taft of the Idoson motor cylinder company, he had developed a new technique by blowing cold air through the castings while they were still hot it had the effect of hardening the surfaces. The barrels were made from cast iron. The bronze head is probably the main distinguishing feature that most people remember about the manxman engine. Later excelsior would develop a system were by an iron sleeve could be inserted into an aluminium casting. This was done using an oven and a deep freeze. So much of what we take for granted today in cylinder construction was started at kings road, in very rudimentary conditions. These two new techniques would help to greatly reduce bore wear and cut down on oil consumption. Now in the main factory work shop production Manager Vic Hawkins would take over the day to day assembly of road going versions of the Manxman's. While the engines for these machines would be built under the stewardship of factory foreman Tommy Wildeman. Unfortunately just as the manxman was to take up its pride of place in production line at kings road disaster struck.

Eric walker called Tyrell Smith and Alan Bruce into his office on the 7th of April 1939. The second world war was approaching fast and excelsior had been given a number of government contracts to fulfil. This would mean that all work on the works racers had to stop forth with and Manxman production would be suspended. This was a devastating blow to Alan Bruce.

A fine example of an 1930s manxman

The manxman was only in production a short time but it is still very much a sort after machine even today. As you can see from its classic styling they were the light weight sports bikes of their day.

The end of manxman production at the Excelsior works would not spell the end of the race team or the manxman quite yet.

Tryell smith together with Alan Bruce decided to set up a syndicate to produce the 500cc racer them selves. Contacting the various manufactures of engine parts and then approaching Eric Walker with the offer to buy all remaining 500cc engines and spares. Eric walker took them up on their offer. As did the companies supplying the components. These included Hepworth and Grandage who under took much of the machining of castings and Beans industries who made many components. Castings for the manxman were made largely by High duty alloys including the piston.

On this page I have placed a copy of an advertisement from the July 1937 issue of the motorcycle.

Before the second world war had chance to start the 500 cc special was taken out for one last time in the 1939 TT. The syndicate would race the machine with engine number GJD99 built by Terrell smith and built into a rear plunger frame of the type used by the 250 cc Manxman roadster. This would be the only Manxman 500 to have this type of frame. Initially things looked good for the bike but with ten laps still to go a carburettor fault caused the engine to flood and so the special manxman had to be withdrawn from the race. A sad end to what looked like a very promising future.

In may of 1939 Alan Bruce had the sprung special shipped to Australia were it still remains today at the Robert Howson museum in Perth Westerner Australia.

The last machines to be tested at the excelsior works before the war were to be two strokes this job was undertaken by Neville Hall. Bruce and Tyrell smith would go onto work for the British Air plane company as developers for their engines.

Sadly the store containing all of the manxman components and drawings was bombed during the war and ever thing was lost. So the Manxman never was re-manufactured after the war. Even so there are still many fine examples still around today thanks to enthusiasts. The manxman had 2 stable mates that Excelsior had produced along side the manxman at the same time. These machines were built with traditional push rod type engines, as with the manxman these machines were still built to a very high standard. They were called the Saxon and the Norseman. The styling was very close to that of the manxman giving the machines that familiar Excelsior roadster look.

Of course the Manxman model might have been the most popular machine to come out of the race inspired stable, but it was just one of several race inspired machines produced at this time by Excelsior in kings road Birmingham.

Among the other machines built with speed in mind was a machine built for an attempt at the land speed record.

The silver comet was to be ridden by Joe Wright. The bike had a JAP super charged engine fitted into an excelsior built frame and the streamlining of most of the bike in sheet steel panelling. The v twin engine was an ohv type with dimensions of 80x99mm bore and stroke respectively. It had heavy weight web front forks, a bevel driven magneto, a twin feed pilgrim pump and superchargers. The rider himself also wore steam lined clothing and helmet. The recesses on the tank were the riders knees were to tuck into tightly were fitted with soft rubber pads to help absorb the vibrations.

The frame was of standard construction using the excelsiors works standard 1 1/6 inch tubing. The construction was of the single seat tube type. The bike had a 2 speed Burman gearbox with a clutch capable of handling up to 120 bhp. The gear changing was by means of a rear facing foot pedal. Long and thin in profile the bike had appeared. The tank could hold 3 ½ gallons of petrol and in a slit compartment a gallon of oil. The tank and tin wear were to be all plain nickel plated. The only sign-age on the bike was a red excelsior rectangle badge on the tank.

Developed to a proved 100bhp at 5400 rpm the JAP engine used standard parts through out. Tuning was made on the engine to expect 11psi from the power plus supercharger. It would be mounted forward of the engine and be driven by 5/8 x 3/8 inch chain from the engine sprocket via a face cam shock absorber, similar to the one used on the engine its self. The carburettor was an Amal car type fitted bellow the supercharger. There were four oil pumps to guarantee a good lubrication of all moving parts. The twin feed pilgrim pump driven off the rear cam shaft fed the big end and back of the front cylinder. The front pump took care of the front of the front cylinder and the two remaining pumps took care of the supercharger driven via the blower rotor shaft. Preliminary testing of the comet was carried out at Montlhery in France this was found to be satisfactory. Reaching 163 mph on one run it looked like the machine had good potential. Unfortunately around this time problems started to manifest them selves. Engine seizures due to piston problems and the supercharger it was decided to call it a day at Montlhery. After two further attempts at getting the machine to a test road with out success the project was abandoned. This machine has now been restored and can now be found at Sammy millers museum in the new forest area of Hampshire in England.

Not all of the competition machines built by Excelsior were for road racing. They would also produce a number of frames for JAP speedway machines. One of which can be found at the Haynes motor museum in Sparkford Somerset England.

One of the race inspired machines to be built by excelsior. I was sent this picture some time ago it had no history with it. But as you can see it does have a marvellous V twin JAP engine. A favourite for many machine builders during the 1930s. Even when the manxman and other race replica machines ceased production during the second world war JAP engines would still be in use. The pre war race pedigree for excelsior would see Excelsior gain 250cc lightweight successes in six major meetings around Europe on their factory built machines. These included first placements in the following meetings. Lightweight TT, Northwest 200, Ulster grand Prix, Swiss Grand Prix, Dutch TT and the Belgian Grand Prix. This was not at all bad for a small company such as Excelsior. The machines that survived the war were still seen to be kept racing in competitions as late as the 1950s.

The war effort

Of course Not all the machines produced at excelsior during the 1930s were of the race pedigree type. By far the most common bikes to come out of excelsior works during the 1930s were small two stroke machines. Among them launched during 1937. we would have found the Autobyke a fore runner to the modern moped. Powered initially by a single speed Villiers junior engine this basic model would later be joined by other models post WW2. These new models would also carry two engines of excelsiors own design. The single speed sprite and 2 speed goblin engines. The little Villiers engine found in the first Autobyke would take an important part in the war effort at Excelsior. Excelsior would still be expected to undertake the manufacture some motorcycles during the war based around the little Autobyke engine.

The chief out put at the Excelsior works during the war would be a small motorcycle known as the welbike. The name for which came from the government backed think tank given the task to help fill some of the gaps in British military transport. At the time the British air force had small transport aircraft so their pay load was limited by their size. Given the remit to create a motorcycle that could be of use to paratroops while still working within the constraints of the size of the aircraft at that time with in the RAF. The organization behind the this project was the special operations executive {SOE}. They had several out stations around the country trying to come up with new ideas and putting them into production. One such out station was station 1X set up at Frythe near welwyn in Hertfordshire. The wel part of welbike derives from Welwyn. Even though this little machine would have been of limited use to the SEO and later by the military. The Welbike was Possibly destined to be the smallest form of transport during the second world war. Of more use as a propagandist tool than a useful resource. Still all said and done this little engineering gem did see active service at the battle of Arnhem in September 1944. As well as at Aubin-sur-mer on D day the 6th of June 1944. it is also document that a welbike was used in Malay during the period of the Japanese surrender.

Well I think that's enough about its war time exploits. Now a description of the Welbike is in order. I will give the following description based on the first prototype mk1. Even though there were only 6 of this model produced I think it will give an insight into the concept behind the bike. Original design work for the mk1 welbike was carried out by Harry Lester and H L Taylor. This early prototype was conceived to be used by the SOE but they declined the offer as they felt that the little motorcycle would not be of any benefit to their operations. So the welbike was offered instead to the paratroops who excepted them. The simple duplex 5/8 inch frame was constructed by having 2 tubes come up from the rear wheel to the head stock and then back along the top of the stock to the rear wheel. The frame was re-enforced with steel plates under the engine and top and bottom of the seat pillar supports. All joints were welded. Front forks were of the bicycle type and the front wheel had no brake. The rear wheel incorporated a 4 inch drum brake that was foot operated by means of a pedal on the right hand side of the machine. Both tires were 12 .5 inches x 2.25 inches. Powered by a 98cc 1939 Villiers junior Deluxe engine. This little engine had been developed by Villiers in 1937 for use in the auto bike. Even so the engines for the welbike were redeveloped to give more punch. The inlet port had been enlarged and the crankcase heightened. The engine had been originally designed by George H Jones. The petrol tanks on the welbike were suspended either side of the top front portion of the frame and were pressure fed to the carburettor by means of a hand pump. Similar to the system found on oil lamps and blow torches of this period. The left hand tank incorporated a pressure release valve.

Total fuel capacity was 6.5 pints of premixed petrol and oil. The extra work on the well bike had been designed by J.R.V.Dolphin he was a lieutenant commander in the airborne regiment. Who was attached to Welwyn. The dimensions of the container in which the welbike was packed was 12"x15"x51". Room for a parachute was at the top of the container.

While the bottom had a crash pan built in to absorb the shock on landing. It is stated that a trained paratrooper was said to be mobile in 11 seconds. To do this amazing feat in agility he would first have to take the bike out of its container by releasing the 2 clips on the centre of the canister.

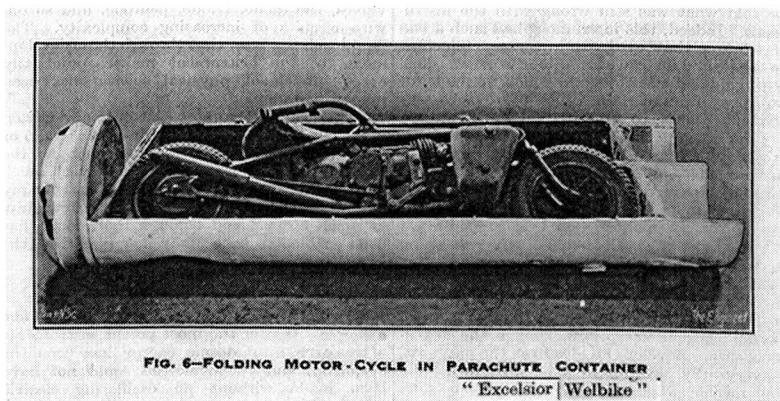

FIG. 6—FOLDING MOTOR-CYCLE IN PARACHUTE CONTAINER
" Excelsior | Welbike "

" Excelsior | Welbike "

FIG. 5—" WELBIKE " FOLDING MOTOR-CYCLE READY FOR USE

Once the bike was out first the seat would have to be raised up until the locking device that was spring loaded clicked into place. Then the handle bar stem would be brought up forward until it locked. Finally the handle bars would be folded out and locked into place with a knurled nut. Then he would have to pressurizes the tank and start the machine. A lot to do in just 11 seconds. The idea was to use the Welbike to get the troops as far from the drop zone as quickly as possible. Designed to keep the weight down as far as possible the welbike weighed in at only 70 pounds. Later a generator version would be developed using a dynamo in the frame this model was called the Wel-charger. The last batch of 1240 welbikes to leave Excelsior were given the war department numbers C5153414-C5154654. After the war excelsior would supply their own engines to Brockhouse engineering who would develop the Welbike into a folding scooter known as the Corgi.. A total production run of 3641 Welbike machines was recorded completed by excelsior by the end of the war. Though it is believed that only around 200 are still surviving today.

With the war excelsior had gained a full engineering work shop with many new machine tools. So after the war the company would find that for the first time in its history engine building in house was a possibility. Starting with a copy of the Villiers junior engine in 1947 the company would go on to develop many engines of its own. So with peace would come new horizons and new goals. Even though the manxman would never be built again, excelsior would bring about a change of concept with regards to light weight motorcycles. Incorporating much of the knowledge they had gained during the war years.

Post war years

The first new machine to leave the kings road works after the war would be the improved Autobyke. As mentioned previously the engine used on the welbike would not just find a home in the little Corgi folding bike, but also in the Auto-cycles to be produced by Excelsior. There would be 4 models available from Excelsior using two stroke single cylinder engines either manufactured by Villiers engines of Wolverhampton or Excelsior own engines.

The engines were denoted by the manufacturers prefix on each Autobyke model. As follows The S1 model had an Excelsior sprite single speed engine fitted. The G2 model had an Excelsior Goblin 2 this engine was a two speed model. Villiers engines were also fitted and were numbered in the same way. VI denoting single speed and V2 a two speed machine. All of the engines had a displacement of 98cc. With a bore and stroke of 50mm. The frames were all of bicycle type with rigid rear frame and elasticated suspension on the front forks. Autobyke engines were mounted before the pedal gear. The gears were selected by using a lever on the top of the petrol tank in the case of the 2 speed models. Throttle control was by handle bar mounted lever that could be left set in one position. The magneto generator could produce 21 watts that supplied the current for the engine as well as a direct feed light set. Front braking was by a 4 inch shoe brake while the rear had a back pedal type brake that was incorporated in the rear wheel. There was no speedometer fitted as standard only as an optional extra. Top speed was under 30 miles per hour. So it was not necessary to have one fitted by law. Priced at between £57.3 shillings and £69.17 shillings these were affordable machines. Best suited to level running the Autobyke could manage some gentle gradients with what was jokingly called light pedal assistance. As the machine weighed in at 130 pounds I can only surmise that it would be hard work for the rider on a steep hill or a longer gradient. Produced from 1937 until 1957 this little machine proved a versatile member of the Excelsior range.

Along side the Autobyk an unusual little bike known as the minor. Available in two models the M1 of 98cc incorporating the goblin engine found on the Autobyk, with the addition of a foot change two speed gearbox. And the M2 with a larger 125cc engine. The M1 had a bore and stroke of 50mm while the M2 was 56mm bore and 50mm stroke.

These little motorcycles had steel tube frames and pressed steel front forks. Front and rear tires were 19 inch by 2.5 inch incorporating 4 inch drum brakes. The saddle was low slung to give a good ridding position and easy steering. The 125 cc model came with a smiths illuminated speedometer, as non was required on the 98cc model by law this model would come without a speedometer unless the customer requested one to be fitted. Both machines had a dry weight of 135lbs.

The Autobyke's and the Minor's were to offer the public a chance to see that Excelsior were capable of producing engines in house now and this little 98cc engine would soon be joined by others.

By 1949 excelsior were ready to launch their next machine with an engine built at kings road. This time the engine and the machine would both be entirely new.

A 250 class machine with a new vertical twin two stroke engine. Described in motorcycle journals at the time as a modern smooth two stroke machine. The new model would be known as the Talisman twin. This machine would represent a leap forward for British light weight motorcycles.

1961 version of the Talisman Twin. TT7

even though this machine is a later model the engine appearance changed very little from the one found in earlier models. With the exception of the cylinder barrels that grew larger thinning. The earlier models were also a lot more light weight in appearance as well as their over all build weight. The TT1 series also only came with a Siamese exhaust fitted. Were as these later models had twin exhausts fitted. While still retaining the beautiful egg shaped engine casting on the left hand side of the machine. This casting also had the Excelsior name embossed with in it. The other side of the engine had the magneto housing and Albion gear box housing with the gear selector mechanism. Later machines had a lot more in the way of tin wear. As you will see when comparing this machine with the one on the 1951 advert on the next page.

Every effort was made to help the Talisman owner keep his machine in good road worthy condition. Including using the motorcycle media. Features in motorcycle magazines were an excellent way to drum up interest in the Talisman.

Now more about the specifications of the machine in detail.

Each cylinder of the 247 cc vertical twin engine had a stroke of 62 mm and a bore of 50mm. The crank case came in three parts housing the crank, flywheel and ignition unit. Supporting the crank were five bearings four ball and one roller. The roller was found at the flywheel end of the crank. Big ends were supported by double row roller bearings. As for the small ends they only had brass bushes with fully floating gudgeon pins. The engine had aluminium pistons each having two piston rings. The cylinder barrels were of cast iron and the cylinder heads of aluminium. A single Amal carburettor supplied the mixture to the cylinders via communal induction. Except on the later sports models when each cylinder had its own carburettor. There was a choice of Ignition units either wico-pacy or miller. This unit also supplied the lighting and charged the six volt battery. The Albion four speed gear box was bolted on to the rear of the crank case giving the engine a look of unit construction. Gear shift was by means of a foot controlled lever. Gear changing was helped by the use of a two plate cork insert clutch that was also rubber mounted. A double endless Primary chain joined the crank to the clutch and ran in a bath of oil. This engine was fitted into a new frame built of single loop steel tubing on the standard model and double loop tubing incorporated in the sports version. The frame also supported a centre stand and plunger type rear suspension units supplied by Girling. Suspension was complemented by telescopic front forks. Distance was no object for the Talisman has it had a big three gallon tank. Later a special 328cc version the S9 would be launched but it believed that this model never gained the popularity of the earlier 247cc machine.

The S9 would in fact be the final incarnation of the Talisman. Fitted with the engine used for the Berkeley car. With twin carburettors and an enclosed rear end, with larger brakes than the earlier 250cc models.

The after sales service was excellent as it was possible to exchange a faulty engine at the kings road works for a refurbished engine held by excelsior or if you wished you could have your own engine refurbished in house by excelsior. Something you would be hard pressed to achieve with today's Japanese, Chinese dominated market.

Excelsior had stolen the march on Villiers with their talisman engine. unfortunately they failed to capitalize on this advantage so when six years later Villiers would bring out their 2T engine other manufacturers would soon be in a position to offer a two stroke twin machine to rival the Talisman.

lay out of bottom end of Berkeley engine designed by Excelsior. Note the Dynastarter unit on the left hand side.

During 1950 the excelsior range were priced as follows.

	Cash price	purchase tax	total price
Model 50/S1 98cc De-luxe Autobyk	£45 0 0	£12 3 0	£57 3 0
model 50/G2 98cc super Autobyk	£ 55 0 0	£14 17 0	£69 17 0

model 50/U1 125cc Universal {direct lighting}	£72 13 6	£19 12 6	£92 6 0
Model 50/U2 125 cc Universal {rectified lighting}	£77 13 6	£20 19 6	£98 13 0
Model 50/R1 197cc Roadmaster {direct lighting}	£81 3 6	£21 18 4	£103 1 10
Model 50/R2 197cc Roadmaster {rectified lighting}	£86 3 6	£23 5 4	£109 8 10
Model 50/TT1 250cc Talisman Twin	£113 3 6	£30 11 2	£143 14 8

compared to the prices they fetch today they were very reasonably priced. Even so only lucky people would own a Talisman then as wages on the hole were quite low.

As you can see the evil spectre of Tax raised the purchase price quite considerably. Something the company would take into consideration more fully in later years. Considering that Excelsior had come out of the second world war with little more than the work shops. They had by now built up a very good new line in machines in what was a relativity short period of time. As in the companies past Excelsior would soon expand this initial range even further to include more home grown engines as well as machines.

By 1951 excelsior would list seven models in that years catalogue.

One of the new models being the 122cc universal model. This bike had a Villiers mark 10 D engine. Available in two models Denoted as the U1and the U2 models. The single port engine had a 50mm bore and a 62 mm stroke. Each version had a 3 speed gear box with foot change mechanism. A cork inserted 2 plate clutch with endless primary drive chain run in a oil bath. Flat top alloy piston with a detachable cylinder head. Ball bearings on the main shaft and roller bearings to the big end. Petrol oil lubrication to the engine was via a Villiers4/5 double lever type carburettor. The spark plug used in the universal was a lodge H14. The difference between the two machines would be the U1 came with a direct Villiers lighting set or U2 with a rectifier battery system from millers. The engines were fitted into an excelsior sprung frame. Front forks were telescopic and were of excelsiors own manufacture. All topped with a 21/2 gallon petrol tank. Around the same time the road-master model was launched. The only difference being the 197cc Villiers 6E engine. With a Villiers single lever ¾ type carburettor. As well as these road machines there would also be small numbers of excelsior speedway machines built at this time with JAP engines. These three road models would continue to be part of excelsiors main production until 1953. When more new models would join the range beside them.

Among the new models to come in 1953 would be more machines with fitted Villiers engines. Including the consort.

The consort was intended as a replacement for the by now ageing auto-cycle range. This light weight single would go on to be the main bread and butter machine for excelsior over the next decade. The little 98cc two stroke would prove an invaluable work horse for many people. Fitted with a Villiers 4f two speed engine and constructed as a simple rigid frame model for almost all of its production life.

Gear change on the consort was by way of a handle bar mounted lever similar to a air mixture lever found on many bikes of this era. Though the junior type carburettor was operated by a throttle twist grip on the end of the right side of the handle bar. Unlike its predecessor the Autobyke with a lever mounted on the handle bars. This of course gave the consort a much wider power band than the earlier Autobyke.

Developing at 4000 rpm 2.8 HP the engine was quite nippy for its day. Gear box ratios were 1.54 to 1 and 1to 1. later models would be up graded when they would also be sold in kit form to include a Villiers 6 F engine that had a 3 speed foot change gearbox built into the engine. The wrights saddle was mounted on springs and the frame was constructed in a sprung manner but had no suspension units in early models. Lighting was by direct feed from the magneto as there was no battery or rectifier fitted to the consort 4F. A cylindrical tool box was bolted on the down tube under the seat. Front forks on the 4F were girder type only being replaced in the late 1950s by the telescopic type of excelsiors own manufacture.. Even when excelsior had updated the consort there were many requests by customers wishing to buy consorts with the old girder type forks. So a special batch of machines with girder forks had to be built. This was due in no small part to the price increase on the modernized models. The older 4F model had sold around 10,000 units a year easily excelsiors top selling model. Ironically it turned out that by modernizing the consort and the subsequent price rise excelsior had lost sales. The last consort was manufactured in 1963 and was believed to have been sold in kit form. This was to alleviate the customer from the purchase tax and to trim the price of the machine a little in the hope that sales would once again raise back up to their previous position.. I once owned an early Consort with girder forks it was quit a neat little bike. That was light and a joy to ride. Except possibly the brakes they left a lot to be desired.

But for a sixty year old machine I guess they were on par with the consorts contemporaries of the time.

Here is an early Consort note the very simple lines of the machine. Built for a price and serving the company longer than any other model produced at Kings road. An example of a simple solution is sometimes the best solution.

As mentioned earlier the final example of the Consort to leave Kings road. Was in kit form. An ingenious idea that would have saved the company had it worked. Now days with the internet and fast delivery services it properly would have stood a better chance of success. But unfortunately even the best ideas can end up on the rocks of time. The next picture shown is of the advertisement used for the later kit bikes. A design giving the final models a more rounded and sturdy look.

Advert for kit build DIY bike.

The next model known as the Skutabyk was in fact the Consort dressed up in tin wear.

This clumsy looking machine did suit a purpose in that it offered the rider a modicum of protection from the elements and the oil from the engine. Looking at the Skutabyk I would say the extra weight of the tin wear must have slowed the machine down considerably. As the Consort was never the fastest bike in the world to start with.

As you can see in the next picture the Skutabyk did served a use full roll. Keeping the riders legs covered from road wash in the wet and engine oil contamination.

15 NOVEMBER 1956

Comprehensive shielding is employed on the Excelsior Skutabyk

1956 SKUTABYK

By the end of 1953 the consort would be joined by a new machine with a 147cc excelsior engine. The new model named the Courier. Utilising many of the parts found on the other universal models with the exception of the engine that was to be built in house. This engine would later in 1958 be super ceded by the Villiers 30 c engine. Fitted with a Villiers S type carburettor. The Courier model numbers would be known as the U8 when fitted with direct lighting and the U8R with rectified lighting. Once again the new machines would have excelsior telescopic front forks.

By now the company was in the hands of the grand sons of Reginald Walker Geoffrey and Denis Walker under the trade name of the Excelsior motor co. Ltd. And so in 1959 these models would become the U9 and the U9R though there would be very little change between the models. Girling rear suspension units were fitted to the later models. By 1961 the universal models would have the Villiers 31c engine fitted.

Becoming the U10 and the U10R respectively. Total dry weight was 200-231 lbs respectively.

Drawing of early road master.

197 c.c. "ROADMASTER"
Model R.2

In 1954 the road master with a new Villiers 8E engine would make an appearance. With a sprung frame with a swinging arm at the rear. Constructed as all excelsior frames were at this time using the braised lug system. Suspension units used on the Road master were identical to those used on the earlier Talisman models. The engine had a bore of 59 mm and a stroke of 72mm. Two models were again available the R1 that had direct wiring lighting and the R2 that had magneto with rectifier and battery. Both models had a 6 pole Villiers magneto each of the machines were wired differently.

The spark plug used in the Road master model was a lodge HH14. Even the bulbs used in the Road master were identical to those used in the universal models. As both machines had identical magnetos. Early models had a 3 position lighting switch fitted but later models were fitted with a 4 position switch. The 4th position was a direct feed so if your battery was flat you still had lights to headlamp and rear light of the machine. A very use full idea. The magneto would produce 6v 12amp/hour passing through a selenium type rectifier to charge the battery. Total dry weight for these new models was 215lbs.This model would also be joined by the Codex in later years. changing the Villiers 30 c engine to a 12 D. this gave the little Codex a 122cc 3 speed engine. Bore and stroke was 50mm and 62mm respectively. Fitted with a Villiers S9 carburettor. full lighting was available with the Codex as the Villiers magneto had ample power. Frame was a duplex type manufactured by Excelsior. Front and rear wheels were 19 inches x 2.25 inches and the machine had a one and three quarter gallon petrol tank.

An excellent example of a later Road master.

So there you have it the 1950s was a time for the utility motorcycle a type of machine that suited Excelsior well.

All in all the company had done very nicely out of the post war era. Even if to start with they could only offer a limited range of machines. By the end of the 1950s the company had pulled of another of its growth spurts. Stating the next decade with a very respectable range of motorcycles as well as other products. So we move on to some of those other products to be found at kings road.

Other Avenues open to Excelsior

As well as complete machines Excelsior also offered to supply engines to other manufactures. Among the engines offered were variants on the Talisman engine.

The in line triple developed in 1956 by excelsior for use in micro cars is probably the most out stand achievement to leave kings road after the second world war. Ostensibly designed with the Berkeley B60 sports car in mind but also used by other manufacturers for other applications.

Based around the 328cc talisman special engine with an additional cylinder of 58mm bore and 62mm stroke. Set up as a transfer port type of engine fed by 3 Amal monobloc carburettors.

The crankcase comprised of 4 sections an end housing at the primary chain end and 2 further centre sections. With a n end cover housing the Siba Dynastarter. This unit was used as a engine starter generator and low tension make and break assembly to service all three ignition coils.

The crank shaft was unusual in being a built up assembly mounted on 4 roller and 3 ball bearings.

There was a synthetic rubber seal set between each crankcase compartment. Firing order for the cylinders was a straight forward 123. the crank throws were 120 degrees.

Each of the 3 connecting rods were solid forgings. With a double row of uncaged roller bearings for each of the big ends. The engine was assembled by first assembling the first throw and connecting rod into the first two halves of the first crank case as a single unit. The next crank half is then keyed onto the end of the first with its crank pin driven in tight. The other half of this sub unit is then slid into place. Using no.6 witney keys to locate each half of the crank journals and then locked on place with a sleeve type nut. This nut was locked in place by peening the thread. The last cylinder could then be assembled. Each of the flat top pistons can then be fitted. Followed by the barrels of cast iron and light alloy heads. These could then be assembled. There is no head gasket employed as a air tight seal is obtained by use of a narrow ring around the cylinder bore. The spark plugs were inclined away from the exhaust ports. Transmission was via a Albion 4 speed gear box. As in the standard talisman engine with the addition of a reverse gear..primary drive chain was a 1/8 pitch duplex roller type. To a multi plate clutch that ran in a bath of oil. No cooling fan was deemed necessary as the exhaust pipes faced forward of the engine giving all necessary cooling. The basic engine weighed in at 98lbs.length of the unit was 21inches easily small enough to fit transversely into the Berkeley.

Berkeley were undoubtedly the main recipient for these triples but other smaller companies were also using them and other Excelsior engines. Among them special motorcycles built by individuals like the EMC built by David Blanchard in 1963.

Blanchard had already made a name for himself with previous creations, including a water cooled twin. By building this triple master piece he excelled himself. Based around an EMC frame and an Excelsior triple engine it was quit a rare piece of manipulative engineering.

He found out that Excelsior were offering their 492cc triple engines formerly built with the Berkeley car in mind for £100. As the engine had a claimed out put of 30bhp and came equipped with a Siba Dynastart he thought it would be ideal for his next project. His first major obstacle came as soon as he offered the engine up to the frame. The rear chain line was way off. His answer was to fit a second Burman gearbox to the machine and take his power from that box. He completed this task by cutting two sets of plates that he finished by hand. Using one to mount the engine to the rear of the frame and the other mounted the extra Burman box to the bottom mounting bolt. This gave him independent means to service either of the boxes when kneed arises. The drive was taken from the power unit to the secondary unit was by outrigger shaft with a sprocket. Both gear boxes were four speed. The left box was left permanently in first gear were as the gears in the Burman box were changed in the normal way. The reverse gear was also still incorporated in the motorcycle. As the engine had originally been built with the Berkeley car in mind. His next task was to find a home for the massive 12v 17 amp hour car battery needed to run the Siba Dynastart system. This was done by the fabrication of a platform constructed from light alloy beneath the seat. Synchronization of the carburettors was carried out through a system of rods and springs devised by Blanchard himself. This gave him a reasonable chance of a light throttle control. He stuck with the 3 carburettor lay out as he was unable to find a single carburettor that could give good over all performance. The exhausts were custom made with the 3 cylinders feeding into an expansion box via stub exhausts with a single outlet exhaust from this chamber. The frame had already come with a Clamil sprung hub that he decided to keep. The front wheel had a 7 inch BSA hub brake to help the bike cope with the expected turn of speed. The fuel tank a whopper was capable of holding 5 gallons. Finished in red and two tone Grey this machine was a beautiful sight. By today's standard the top end of 85 mph wont seem that much but for a two stroke engine designed in the 1950s this machine would or could have save Excelsior from extinction had they had the for thought to create a similar machine them selves. As any one who witnessed the triples produced by Suzuki and Kawasaki during the 1970s would testify too.

The Talisman engine was probably the most versatile post war engine developed by Excelsior.

Other manufacturers to use talisman engines in their machines included small light car manufacturers.

Such as Seymour's of the wharf in Totnes Devon. They are believed to have produced a small number of 3 wheelers using Excelsior Talisman engines as power units. Apart from a single entry about this company this was all I was able to find out about them.

Frisky cars of Wolverhampton were also customers for the Excelsior engines. Manufactures of several models of light car Frisky cars would become invaluable during the petrol rationing brought on by the

Suez crisis during 1956. though initially conceived as a cheep form of transport for the third world. Set up by captain Raymond Fowler formally of the Cairo motor company. Who after fleeing Egypt earlier that year to escape the new dictatorship. Approached Henry Meadows Ltd of Wolverhampton with a plan to develop and build his range of light weight auto mobiles. Meadows was enthusiastic from the start and space was immediately made available to Captain Fowler within the Meadows works. Meadows had previously supplied engines to many auto producers. Including early Excelsior cars at kings road. In 1957 the first prototype frisky was tested. Design work was carried out by Gordon Benson and Keith Peckmore. Development had commenced earlier in July of 1956 a futuristic 2 seated little car with four wheels and gull type doors. Body work was constructed by Vignale of Turin. Fist car was powered by a 250cc Villiers engine. This had 4 speeds forward and a reverse that was obtained by running the engine backwards. Priced at £400 was launched on 11th march 1957.

by June 1957 the new car company was registered as Henry Meadows vehicles Ltd. Convertible and sports models would follow along with the family three a three wheeled car. Several different engines were tried in frisky cars over the next two years. Including the 3 cylinder 492cc Excelsior engine in a prototype sports model the frisky sprint. By 1958 the company had changed names again to frisky cars Ltd. Not long after this the company folded because of financial difficulties. The Frisky sprint never made it past the prototype stage. So a new market for the new triple engine was lost before it had begun. There were at this time several micro cars being manufactured in Britain. Excelsior had supplied engines to most of them at some point.

Fairthorpe of Chalfront St peter in Buckingham-shire also had a go at producing a light sports car using an Excelsior engine. Called the Atom. The prototype was designed by by Air Vice Marshall Donald Bennett. Manufactured from GRP [reinforced glass fibre]. Although there was a lot of interest from America the project never was a great success. So it was dropped in favour of cars with larger capacity engines mainly based around BSA engines. Berkeley however were undoubtedly the largest single buyer for the excelsior micro car engines.

Founded in 1956 by Charles Panter and Laurie Bond at the Berkeley caravan factory in Biggles-wade Bedford shire. The Berkeley coach works had been one of largest producers of caravans in Europe when Laurie bond approached Charles panter the owner about setting up a sports car factory. The company had become expert in the use of GRP manufacture. So Berkeley welcomed the chance to get involved in the auto mobile industry.

Models included the T60, T60/4, SE328, SE492, B95 and the B105. Engines used in the Berkeley range were between 322 and 692 cc. All of motorcycle origin.

The Excelsior engines favoured were the new triple cylinder models as denoted by the model prefix of SE. Front wheel drive was standard on models produced between 1956 and 1960. the body panels were made up in three sections. The floor the tail and the nose. Light weight but strong and durable the little sports cars were soon to prove very popular. It was said that Stirling moss even rid in one at a meeting held at Goodwood in September of 1956. Even though The new car had only been launched at the London car show held earlier that year at Earls court. Unfortunately by 1960 the almost total collapse of the caravan market that year had left the Berkeley company on the edge of bankruptcy.

Laurie Bond tried to save the sports car from the bankruptcy but to late in the day to succeed. So with the inevitability of the collapse of Berkeley came the end of the road for the little sports car. Along with it came the end of another avenue for supplying engines and the much kneed cash that came with it for Excelsior.

One thing that is obvious from all this is the fact that unlike the common consensus bounded around that the British motorcycle industry had been found resting on their laurels some what. Leading to the collapse of the British motorcycle industry when they were confronted by the great Japanese motorcycle invasion. Is totally untrue at least in Excelsiors case they were found wanting when it came to market strategy. As we have seen as well as the supply of engines for their own use they were more than capable of supplying engines to other producers as well as other lines in auto parts produced at kings road for many customers.

These included the walker range of assemblies Cables, seats industrial trolleys to mention a few.

As well as the air cooled two stroke twin and triple engines Excelsior also were by now producing a number of water cooled out board engines for use with small boats. It is also believed that the excelsior talisman engine was the base used by the British Anzani company for their Tritton 2 and Tritton3 outboard engines. Along with their own Scooter fan cooled engine. For the monarch scooters produced by Excelsior in house.

I will cover this particular engine in greater detail over the next few pages. Along with the machines Excelsior designed the engine for.

The Monarch was a 150cc scooter the internals for which were built by Excelsior almost entirely in house including the engine.

The exceptions being the Albion gearbox and plastic panelling that were DKR manufactured.

As the monarch had originally been a DKR design.

The DKR company had been set up at Pendeford airport at Wolverhampton by Barry Day, Noah Robinson and Cyril Kieft.

Scooters were designed by Cyril Kieft and constructed at their factory in Neaches lane Wolverhampton. Original machines were fitted with a square bore fan cooled Villiers engine.

The Monarch was the long awaited replacement for the by now ageing skutabyke. Probably the best example of the short lived monarch scooter was to be the Mk2. Launched in 1960 and available with or without electric starter. The old heavy metal panelling had now Gone. Replaced by the modern reinforced plastic. Greatly helping to reduce the overall weight of the machine. The electric start model came with a Dynastart system and 12volt electrics. Backed up by 2 6volt 12 amp hour batteries.

The all new excelsior fan cooled 150cc two stroke engine was pacifically designed for use in the Monarch. This was carried out by utilising an existing design used in the 147 cc courier motorcycle. This was achieved by enlarging the and deepening the finning on the cylinder barrel and inclining the transverse finning towards the light alloy fan mounted on the drive side of the engine. The fan is driven via a drive shaft that is supported by two ball journal bearings. Encased in a light allow casting. On the generator side was another light alloy casting housing either the siba unit or the wico-pacy flywheel type generator. The bore was 53mm and stroke 62mm giving a total capacity of 150cc. Complemented by a zenith auto choke carburettor. The transmission was via a semi unit 3 speed gear box. Manufactured by Albion. Fitted with a 2 plate cork inserted clutch that ran in an oil bath. Gear ratios were 5.0 7.9 and 14.2-1. wheels were constructed using two steel pressings. With a 6 inch front drum brake and 5 inch rear.

Colours that were available were maroon/ivory light green/ivory and blue with ivory. Quite a modern colour scheme. The total weight of the Dynastart model was 260lbs. With ground clearance of 5 ½ inches and seat height of 29 inches. The wheel base was stated as 56 inches. A latex foam filled duel seat gave the rider a comfortable ride. The on the road price for this model was £184 and 10shillings.

The cheaper kick starter model weighed in at 228lbs and was priced at £164 and 10 shillings.

Even thou the Monarch had started of as a re-badged machine. It is very apparent the Excelsior company had put a great deal of work into revamping the machine.

Unfortunately the Monarch was not to be the saving grace that Excelsior had hoped it would be. As its launch coincided with the start of the demise of the company. It isn't known exactly how many Monarchs were produced at kings road, or if any have survived until today. This would be something of great interest to find out one day. The name monarch had been used by the company on two occasions before. Once in the companies pre Excelsior days as the badge for motorcycles built for a large London department store by the Walkers. And later as the companies telegraphic name. It certainly appeared to be a very sturdy machine. Unfortunately it lacked the graceful curves of its Italian rivals. As most of the scooter market at this time was taken up by youthful lads the large practical shape of the monarch didn't appeal to a large enough market to prove a viable proposition. So in a relativity short period of time the model along with some others would be dropped from the range of machines available.

So it is ever more apparent that Excelsior were trying incredibly hard to move their production forward. With more complex engine design work being carried forward to completion, as well as improvements on existing machines with further development work across its range of products. The production included manufacturing of their own front forks. These were assembled during the 1960 by their assembly specialist Percy Jones and his team.

Along side the motorcycles built at 260 kings road Tyseley were a range of industrial trucks. Known as the Pyramid range. There were three main trucks available.

Model 109 dumper truck. This truck had a caring capacity of 7 hundred weight. An 11/4 HP 4 stroke engine was fitted coupled to a 3 speed gearbox. It ran on 16 inch wheels.

Model 102 flat bed truck. This truck had a 38 inch bed length could carry one ton. Came with a choice of 2 engine sizes, the larger giving greater caring capacity.

Model 107 sti'llage truck. This to was a flat bed truck with the addition of a hand pumped hydraulic system. Carry weight up to 1750lbs. Platform measured 48 inches by 24 inches.

These were produced by a special industrial truck division within Excelsior.

On top of the truck division there was also the outboard motor arm of the company manufacturing outboard motors of various designs. Even with these extra lines within the company Excelsior were still struggling to keep their head above water. In the end it would not be down to lack of determination on the part of Excelsior that would lead to the final closure of the works at kings road.

As I mentioned earlier a large per portion of the blame for Excelsiors down fall was to come via a third party that the Excelsior company had become heavily involved with.

The micro car industry was hoped to have been a great savour for the Talisman engine and its derivatives. That was to say so much time effort and expenditure had gone into the triple engine so that the only way Excelsior could hope to even break even over the project would be to have the continued support of companies such as Berkeley. Unfortunately this one bad judgement would prove to be Excelsiors Achilles heel. Before long Excelsior would start to feel real hardship due to the demise of the micro car industry.

As if this problem was not enough for the company to cope with the imminent closure of the Villiers engine plant would have almost certainly been the final nail in the coffin lid. In fact by 1963 all but 3 motorcycle models had been dropped from production as severe cut backs had been implemented in order to try and save the company. Unfortunately two of these models had Villiers engines. Just as they were about to become unavailable.

Known as the CK14 Consort-DE-Deluxe. This machine had a 98cc Villiers 6F engine and came as a kit bike. For the keen DIY builder to build him self.

The other machine also in kit form was the Universal 150cc UK14 model. This also had a Villiers engine. As by now all production of in house Talisman engines had ceased. Only the 147 cc Excelsior engine would be continued, and fitted into the third kit bike the EUK12 universal 150. But they would continued with frame and fork production. Frames were still being manufactured using the braised lug method. As for the front forks they were considered possibly the simplest available on the market at the time.

Excelsior had opted for this method of sales for two main reasons. Firstly to avoid purchase tax on the new motorcycles hence reducing the cost to the purchaser. For example the EUK 12 was priced at just

99 gns. As I mention earlier a good idea but unfortunately it arrived at the wrong time to be a great the success Excelsior had hoped for.

Excelsior had pinned a lot on this venture being a success. This would hopefully lead to the increased machine sales. Something the ailing company was very much in need of.

This method of construction would also reduce the over all man hours that would be spent on each machine within the factory. Giving the company greater scope over all for profit and allowing the ailing company to down size its work force reasonably safely. Unfortunately in the long run this would turn out to be a mistake on Excelsiors part. Because shortly after they had launched the CK 14/ UK 14 Villiers closed down production leaving them with no power plants for two of the new range of machines. If only they had found a way to continued with their own 150 cc engines in the Universal model and the monarch fitted with the adapted 147 engine, they might just have pulled it off. They say the pages of history are littered with good intentions. It was unfortunate that Excelsior took what turned out to be the wrong path. The one that would inevitably lead to the companies demise.

So it was that by 1964 Excelsior of Kings road, Tyseley Birmingham would close its factory gates for the last time. It is believed that immediately prior to the start of the final troubles the company employed over 350 staff. What their fate was is not documented but I understand at least a few were employed by other manufactures in the area producing auto spares. As for the design team it is said that Jim smith the last chief of design at the kings road works was offered employment at Triumph motorcycles. The factories final days were over seen by factory manager Harry Rimmer. Who is believed to have acquired the brass factory name plate when he left the premises for the last time along with the last motorcycle to be produced at kings road. One odd foot note in the history of this company is that there were a number of machines registered in 1965, as well as a range leaflet printed for 1965 showing the full range of machines pre kit build days. one can only surmise that the leaflet was ordered some time before the troubles came home to roost. And the printers printed them any way.

Quite who owns the manufacturing rights for the Excelsior name is open to some conjecture. BSA did own the old Excelsior works in kings road for a short time. But this seems to have been an asset stripping exercise on their part. Then in 1963 the Britax group took ownership, they even produced a small trail/road bike during the 1970s that carried the joint Britax/Excelsior badge. This was a short lived production run not to dissimilar to machines the BSA rambler and NVT tracker also produced at that time. All of which followed the same fate. Final products to carry the excelsior motor company name were a new type of car seat belt that locked after rapid deceleration. These were a joint venture within the Britax group.

The old Excelsior works is no longer to be found at kings road, but the former site is easy to find now occupied by a number of small rented industrial units on the junction of Redfern road and kings road Tyseley Birmingham. The industrial estate is called Rovex business park.

Well there you have it a story of engineering, and motorcycle pioneering and a place in the pages of the history of British motorcycle manufacturing. Just what conclusions you reach about the fate of the Excelsior motor company is now down to your own interpretation of this book. I hope that you have found this an interesting journey through time and that you now feel you know a lot more about the company. Now at least Excelsior do stand a chance of finding its rightfully deserved place in the motorcycling history of Britain.

To finish off the book I decided to share a few pictures and prints that I have acquired over the years. So over the next few pages you will find adverts posters and articles about some of the many products to leave the Excelsior factory.

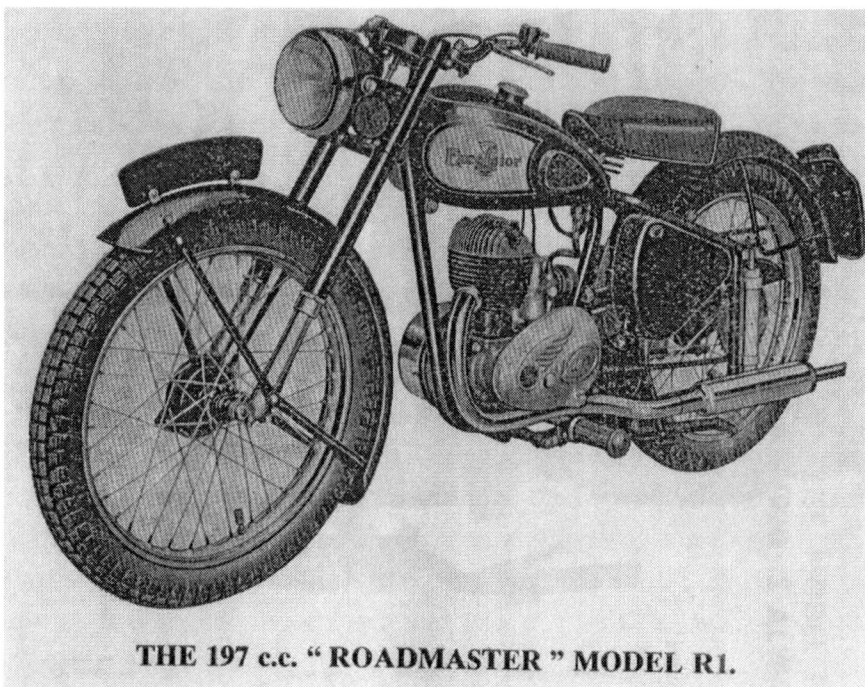

THE 197 c.c. " ROADMASTER " MODEL R1.

An early roadmaster print taken from parts listings.

Light weight trucks as well as motorcycles.

The Talisman featured many times in the motorcycle press.

Here are a two examples.

The Albion 4 speed gearbox a favourite at Excelsior.

TALISMAN TWIN

SEE HOW TOM WILDMAN OF EXCELSIOR STRIPS IT

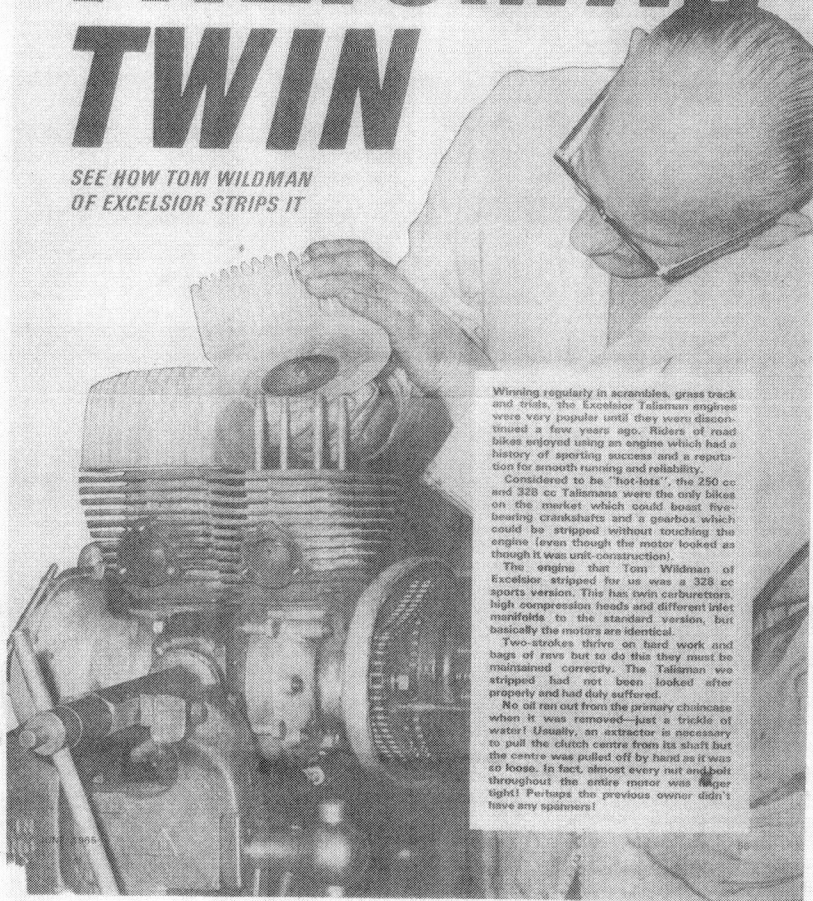

Winning regularly in scrambles, grass track and trials, the Excelsior Talisman engines were very popular until they were discontinued a few years ago. Riders of road bikes enjoyed using an engine which had a history of sporting success and a reputation for smooth running and reliability.

Considered to be "hot-lots", the 250 cc and 328 cc Talismans were the only bikes on the market which could boast five-bearing crankshafts and a gearbox which could be stripped without touching the engine (even though the motor looked as though it was unit-construction).

The engine that Tom Wildman of Excelsior stripped for us was a 328 cc sports version. This has twin carburetters, high compression heads and different inlet manifolds to the standard version, but basically the motors are identical.

Two-strokes thrive on hard work and bags of revs but to do this they must be maintained correctly. The Talisman we stripped had not been looked after properly and had duly suffered.

No oil ran out from the primary chaincase when it was removed—just a trickle of water! Usually, an extractor is necessary to pull the clutch centre from its shaft but the centre was pulled off by hand as it was so loose. In fact, almost every nut and bolt throughout the entire motor was finger tight! Perhaps the previous owner didn't have any spanners!

Engine given a full strip on the Talisman.

Swinging arm suspension and the condor make an appearance.

Advertisement for The Autobyk early forerunner of the moped.

Advertisement for The Autobyk early forerunner of the moped.

Reprinted from "Motor Cycling with Scooter Weekly," June 23 and June 30, 1960

KNOW YOUR ENGINE

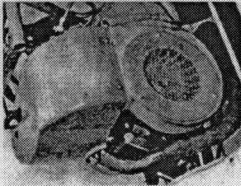

No. X: The 150 c.c. EXCELSIOR Two-stroke

THE 150 c.c. Excelsior two-stroke scooter engine has already gained a splendid reputation for itself in the "Monarch" before the latest version of this unit, which is to be used in a completely new Excelsior machine, full details of which are due to be released in our issue of next week. Excelsior engines have powered motorcycles since the 1920s, and this unit is a typical example of their sturdy construction. Note that a large size Amal fully adjustable Amal carburettor is fitted. It will be seen that the engine is an easy one to work on, all parts being assembled in a straightforward manner. The gearbox used is equally simple and sturdy.

KEY

1. Gear selector mechanism cover.
2. Clutch lifting adjustment cover.
3. Gearchange lever returning bolt.
4. Clutch pushrod operating mechanism.
5. Clutch cable adjuster anchorage.
6. Gear selector actuating mechanism.
7. Final drive sprocket.
8. Amal carburettor.
9. Cooling air ducting.
10. Gudgeon pin and piston.
11. Exhaust port.
12. Transfer port.
13. Voltage control box.
14. Contact breaker mechanism cover.
15. Stator housing cover.
16. Rotor.
17. Flywheels, timing side.
18. Crankpin.
19. Engine mainshaft sprocket and primary chain.
20. Cooling fan.
21. Fan housing intake cover.

The Excelsior engine, as fitted in the current "Monarch" model.

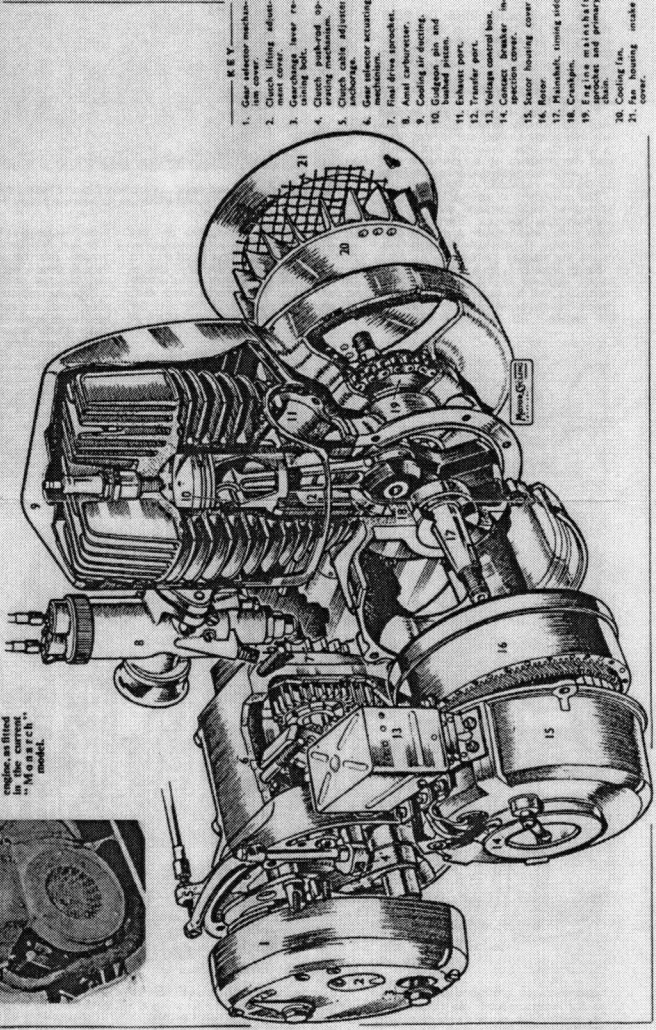

The new monarch engine.

The monarch scooter showed such promise but was not to be.

Reprinted from "Motor Cycling with Scooter Weekly," June 23 and June 30, 1960

spat " panels. These, secured to the main body by patent snap fasteners, shroud the rear wheel more deeply.

For those in search of a slightly less luxurious version, the specification is pared to provide an alternative " Monarch II," with the engine, new frame and advanced glass-fibre construction, but lacking the Siba " Dynastart." In this case " electrics " take the form of a Wipac 6-v.-output generator with rectifier and battery lighting and normal kickstarter equipment.

Extras which are to be available include a windscreen, spare wheel, carrier, wheel embellishers, " Side-spats " and a handlebar mirror, the prices of which will be announced shortly.

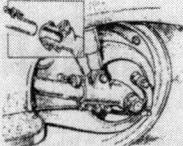

The ingenious telescopic form of the rear suspension arm enables chain adjustment to be made with ease. The chain is fully enclosed in a steel case.

This general arrangement drawing shows clearly that considerable thought has gone into the design, resulting in a pleasant-looking compact machine with simple working parts and the promise of long service

The rear of the body is attached to the chassis by wing nuts, the removal of which permits complete removal of the coachwork which, in turn, provides easy access to the engine. In this view and in the drawing below the optional rear-wheel " Side-spats " are fitted.

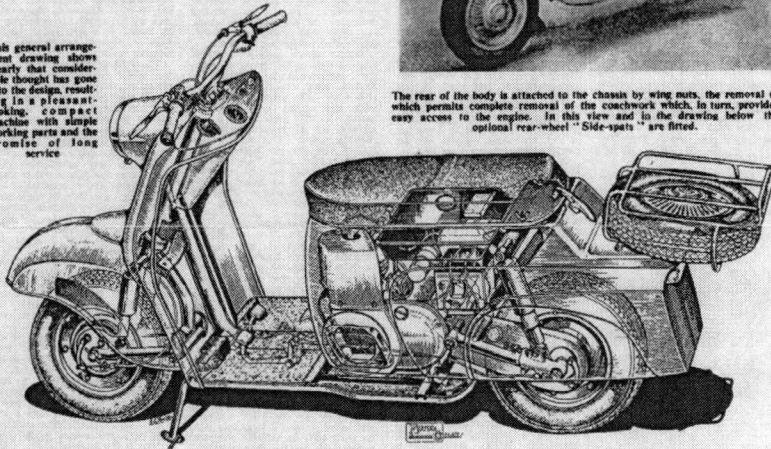

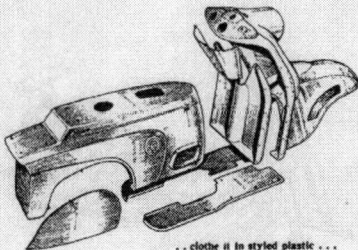

.. clothe it in styled plastic ...

... and you get an extremely handsome machine!

Announcing the NEW

98 c.c. (Model M.1.) and 125 c.c. (Model M.2.) "MINOR"

'Excelsior'
MOTOR CYCLE

- A Minor Model with a Major Performance
- Low in cost — Economical in upkeep
- The ideal utility machine

ABRIDGED SPECIFICATION

ENGINE & GEAR UNIT
EXCELSIOR Two-stroke "Goblin" Mk II Engine, 96 c.c. 50 m/m bore × 50 m/m stroke, and 125 c.c. 56 m/m bore × 50 m/m stroke. Unit construction with 2 speed footchange gear and kick starter. Petroil lubrication. A.M.A.L. Carburetter with twist grip control and strangler for easy starting.

IGNITION & LIGHTING
Miller Flywheel Magneto and 27 watt Direct Lighting Set, with parking light.

FRAME
Built up with high quality weldless steel tube. Exceptionally strong, giving maximum strength and rigidity. Low riding position providing perfect steering control.

FRONT FORKS
Pressed steel with link action and central compression spring. Large bearing surfaces with high tensile steel spindles.

TANK
All steel heavy gauge welded, arranged for Petroil lubrication. Capacity 13½ pints.

WHEELS & TYRES
Internal expanding brakes front and rear. Large section rims built up with heavy gauge spokes. Dunlop tyres 19" × 2.50" diameter.

SADDLE
Large supple top with flexible springs, very comfortable.

HANDLEBARS
Modern "clean" type, adjustable and fitted with twist grip control.

TOOLBOX & EQUIPMENT
Large capacity steel toolbox with full kit of tools, Tyre inflator, Bulb Horn and Licence Holder.

FINISH
Frame parts are rust-proofed and stove enamelled in attractive maroon finish. All chromium plated parts including Exhaust pipe and Silencer are heavily plated.

WEIGHT
With full equipment, 135 lbs approx.

SPEEDOMETER (For machines supplied to Home Dealers) Not compulsory or supplied with any machine under 100 c.c. If required later it can be supplied and fitted by any Excelsior Dealer. The 125 c.c. model is fitted unless otherwise ordered, with a Smith's illuminated, chronometric non-trip speedometer, at an extra charge.

THE EXCELSIOR MOTOR CO. LTD.

Telephone: ACocks Green 1677-8-9   KINGS ROAD, TYSELEY, BIRMINGHAM, 11   Telegrams: Monarch, Haymills

The American this picture was kindly sent to me by its owner in America.

Postcard from the early 1950s depicting the Talisman.

A single ported universal 125 cc. As well as a rare twin ported universal empire model.

1948 excelsior Autobyk with 2 speed goblin engine.
This little engine was probably one of the most versatile engines produced at kings road. Not only fitted to Autobykes but minor models and the Brockhouse corgi.

HURRY! BUILD IT · RIDE IT

independent cheap travel
low initial cost
exciting to build

THE BUILT UP
50 c.c. EXCELSIOR
UNIVERSAL
MODEL EUK 12

99 GNS. ONLY

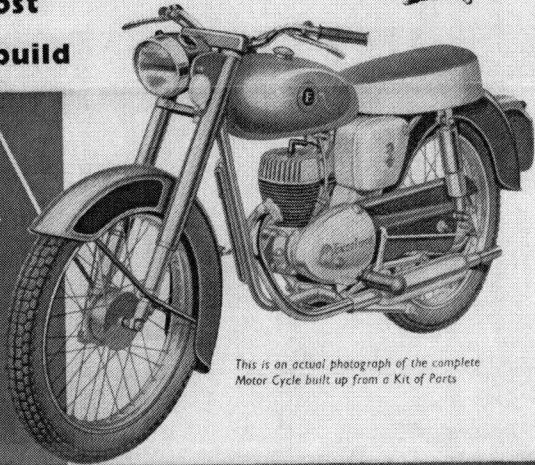

This is an actual photograph of the complete
Motor Cycle built up from a Kit of Parts

ORDER NOW
FOR EARLY
DELIVERY

Order through your local Dealer — or direct

A new and exciting form of building
your own motor cycle

All guaranteed fitment parts

Simple and easy to build

Gives you independent personal travel
at low cost

Not a toy but a full sized standard
Motor Cycle

Detailed assembly instructions supplied
with each Kit

That was the story of Excelsior motorcycles. I do hope that you enjoyed this book and found it interesting. I know I did compiling the facts within its covers. Recent times have seen a greater awareness that Excelsior motorcycles existed. Now more people than ever before are trying to restore tired rusty machines they have found hidden away in old barns and sheds around the world, not just here in the UK. So lets hope that theses machines together with this little book will help the name Excelsior live on for some time to come.

About the Author

After an earlier attempt at telling the story of Excelsior motorcycles. I decided the first book didn't go deep enough into the companies story.

So after much research and work

The new improved book is now available. I have been a life long motorcycle enthusiast.

So the book has been the ultimate

Incarnation of my obsession.

Lightning Source UK Ltd.
Milton Keynes UK
UKOW04f1118041115

262082UK00001B/120/P